Daniel Loskamp

Testing the CAPM on the German Stock Market

GRIN Verlag

Bibliografische Information der Deutschen Nationalbibliothek:

Die Deutsche Bibliothek verzeichnet diese Publikation in der Deutschen Nationalbibliografie; detaillierte bibliografische Daten sind im Internet über http://dnb.d-nb.de/ abrufbar.

Imprint:

Druck und Bindung: Books on Demand GmbH, Norderstedt Germany
ISBN: 978-3-638-67743-1

EUROPEAN BUSINESS SCHOOL
International University Schloß Reichartshausen am Rhein

Seminar Paper

For the seminar on Asset Management

Semester 2005/2006

"Testing the CAPM for the German stock market"

Submission date: 29th of September, 2005

Table of contents

List of figures

List of abbreviations

CAPM	- Capital Asset Pricing Model
FIBOR	- Frankfurt Interbank Offered Rate
NBER	-National Bureau of Economic Research
OLS	- Ordinary Least Square
P/E	- Price/ Earnings
SML	- Securities Market Line

List of symbols

$\hat{\alpha}$	- Denotes the intercept term of the time-series regression
$\hat{\alpha}_P$	- Denotes the intercept term of the time-series regression for any portfolio P
α_i	- Denotes the intercept term of the regression for any asset i
$\hat{\beta}$	- Denotes the slope of the time-series regression
β_i	- Denotes the slope of the OLS regression for any asset i
$\hat{\beta}_P$	- Estimated risk coefficient for any portfolio P
β_{iM}	- Risk coefficient in terms of an asset's market beta
ε_{Pt}	- Error term in the time-series regression for any portfolio P in time t
γ_1	- Average monthly excess return on the market
$\hat{\gamma}_0$	- Denotes the intercept term of the cross-sectional regression
$\hat{\gamma}_1$	- Denotes the slope of the cross-sectional regression
$\bar{e}_P^*$	- Measurement error for any portfolio P
$E(R_i)$	- Expected return on any asset i
$E(R_M)$	- Expected return on the market
$E(R_P)$	- Expected return on any portfolio P
N	- Number of securities in a portfolio
$\overline{R}$	- Average monthly excess return
r	- Correlation coefficient
R_f	- Risk-free rate
R_{ft}	- Risk-free rate in time t
R_i	- Return on any asset i
R_{it}	- Return on any asset i in time t
R_M	- Return on the market
$\overline{R}_M$	- Average monthly excess return on the market
R_{Mt}	- Return on the market in time t
$\overline{R}_{Mt}$	- Average monthly excess return on the market in time t
R_P	- Return on any portfolio P
$\overline{R}_P$	- Average monthly excess return on any portfolio P

$\overline{R}_{Pt}$	- Average monthly excess return on any portfolio P in time t
s	- Standard error
x_{iP}	- The weight of assets in any portfolio P

1 Introduction

1.1 Motivation and Objective

The capital asset pricing model (CAPM) is one of the most important models in financial economics and has a long history of theoretical and empirical investigations.[1] It was developed by William Sharpe (1964) and John Lintner (1965) and offered first insights in how the risk of an investment affects the expected returns, resulting in a Nobel Prize for Sharpe in 1990.[2] The CAPM states that the risk of an asset is measured by the beta of its cash flows with respect to the return of the market portfolio of all assets in the economy.[3] The fact that is so easy to understand underlines the importance of the model and contributes to its success in today's business world. Over 40 years after it was developed, the CAPM is still used in many different fields e.g. to evaluate the performance of a managed portfolio or a mutual fund,[4] assess the risk of a cash flow or estimate the cost of capital of a firm.[5] A recent study states that nearly three fourth of U.S. companies almost always use the CAPM when determining their cost of capital.[6] On top of that it is the preferred asset pricing model in finance and investment courses.[7] Furthermore, one can determine the required rate of return of any risky asset when using the CAPM.[8]

Although the model is widely accepted and practically used as explained above, it is nevertheless far from being perfect as outlined in its record of empirical studies.[9] Generally criticized is on the one hand that the underlying assumptions of the model are very theoretical and thus not able to illustrate reality and on the other one that there are problems in implementing well-founded tests of the model relating to the choice of the right market portfolio.[10] But, the success of the CAPM will remain as long as there is no other model which offers as "[...] powerful and intuitively pleasing predictions about how to measure risk and the relation between risk and return."[11]

---

1 See JAVED (2000), pp. 2f.
2 See PEROLD (2004), p. 3.
3 See JAGANNATHAN/ WANG (1996), pp. 3f.
4 See FAMA/ FRENCH (2004), p. 44.
5 See FAMA/ FRENCH (2004), p. 25.
6 See GRAHAM/ HARVEY (2001), pp. 187-244.
7 See JAGANNATHAN/ WANG (1996), p. 4.
8 See REILLY/ BROWN (2003), p. 238.
9 See ROLL (1977), pp.129-177; BANZ (1981), pp. 3-18; FAMA/ FRENCH (1992), pp. 427-465.
10 See FAMA/ FRENCH (2004), p. 25.
11 FAMA/ FRENCH (2004), p. 25.

The objective of this study is to empirically test the CAPM on the German stock market. Since most of the empirical studies that have been made in the past focus on the U.S. stock market, this paper will try to find out if the results of these U.S. empirical studies can also be shown on the German stock market. Therefore, the goal of this paper is to analyze the relationship between risk and return on the German stock market to find out whether the CAPM holds.

1.2 Course of Exploration

Before the empirical investigation is commenced, a theoretical background is presented that will supply the reader with the required knowledge to understand the CAPM and its implications. Firstly, the model is pointed out in chapter 2 by explaining the underlying concepts and the area of practical applications of the CAPM. Within these explanations the Sharpe-Lintner version, which is also the model to be tested in this paper, and its assumptions are presented. The next section of the paper sums up the critique and the shortcomings of the model.

Chapter 3 will then provide the reader with a brief overview about the literature debate which is connected to the topic of this paper. In order to do so, the main and often cited studies about testing the CAPM and their conclusions are presented firstly, before some previous studies on the German market and their implications are summarized.

The fourth chapter includes the main part of this paper, where the empirical study about testing the CAPM on the German stock market is developed. Section 4.1 describes the data which is being used, before the methodology of the empirical part is explained in detail in the following in order to provide the reader with an overview about how the empirical study has been structured. Section 4.3 describes the results that have been found and analyzes the findings.

Finally, the conclusion is drawn and the results of the paper are summed up in the last chapter.

2 The Capital Asset Pricing Model

2.1 The Model

This study will focus on the Sharpe-Lintner version of the CAPM, which is based on the one period mean-variance portfolio theory of Markowitz.[12] The Markowitz Model assumes that investors are risk averse and only care about risk (variance) and return (mean) of their one-period investment return.[13] Therefore investors choose "[...] mean-variance-efficient [...]"[14] portfolios meaning that they either maximize the expected return, given a certain variance of portfolio return or minimize the variance, given a certain expected return.

To obtain the CAPM in its basic form some assumptions need be fulfilled and are explained in the following. Firstly, investors are risk averse as in the Markowitz Model and evaluate their investment only in terms of expected return and variance of return measured over the same single holding period. The second assumption is that capital markets are perfect meaning that all assets are infinitely divisible, that no transaction costs, short selling restrictions or taxes occur, that all investors can lend and borrow at the risk free rate and that all information is costless and available for everyone. Thirdly, all investors have the same investment opportunity. Finally, all investors estimate the same individual asset return, correlation among assets and standard deviations of return.[15] Based on these assumptions, Sharpe and Lintner developed the following formula, which states that the expected return on any asset i, $E(R_i)$, is the risk-free rate, R_f, plus a premium per unit of beta risk, which is calculated by subtracting the risk free rate from the expected return of the market, $E(R_M)$ and multiplying the result with the risk premium in terms of the asset's market beta, β_{iM}. The latter one is calculated by the covariance of the individual asset returns, R_i, with the market return, R_M, divided by the variance of the market return.

$$E(R_i) = R_f + [E(R_M)-R_f]\,\beta_{iM},\ i=1,\ldots N.$$

Given:

$$\beta_{iM} = \frac{\operatorname{cov}(R_i, R_M)}{\sigma^2(R_M)}$$

The main underlying concept is that assets with a high risk (high beta) should earn a higher return than assets with a low risk (low beta) and vice versa. This seems to be a

---

12 See FAMA/ FRENCH (2004), p. 26.

13 See MARKOWITZ (1952), pp. 77-91.

14 FAMA (1996), p. 441.

very intuitive concept since no investor would be willing to take on more risk if it is not rewarded by a higher expected return. The implication which can be drawn out of this is that all assets with a beta above zero bear some risk and therefore their expected return is above the return of the risk-free rate. As there is only systematic risk in the CAPM world, assets which are completely uncorrelated to the market and thus have a beta of zero should earn a return which is equal to the risk-free rate. This is a fact because only the systematic risk resulting out of economic activity counts in the CAPM, whereas unsystematic risk can be eliminated by using a high degree of diversification. [16] Consequential, there is only one risk-return efficient portfolio, which is also called market portfolio and will be hold by every single investor. Therefore, the investors in the CAPM just have to decide how much to invest in the market portfolio, which has a beta of one and the remainder will be invested in the risk-free rate. Resulting out of that is the securities market line on which all investors will plot their securities in equilibrium. The above mentioned choice of the investor, to put part of their investment into the market portfolio and the other one into the risk free rate, determines the location of the portfolio on the securities market line.[17]

Figure I: The Securities Market Line (SML)

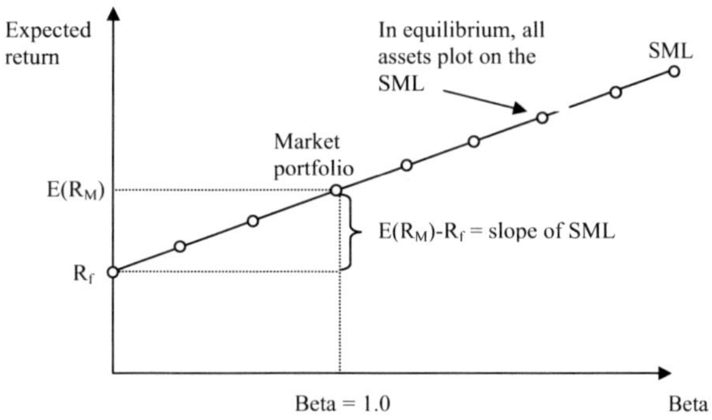

Source: Following PEROLD (2004), p. 18.

As intuitive as the model is, all the unrealistic assumptions evidently lead to critique, which will be pointed out more detailed in the following.

---

[15] See PEROLD (2004), pp. 15f.
[16] See SHARPE (1964), p. 441.

2.2 Criticism and Shortcomings

Although, widely used in business as pointed out in the beginning there are many aspects of the CAPM that have been criticized in the past.[18] One point to mention here is that the empirical record of the model is quite poor, implying that nearly all recent studies reject the model's validity in the real world.[19] Empirical evidence has been found that one of the main conclusions of the CAPM, that the return of an asset solely depends on its correlation to the market (beta), does not hold true in reality since several studies show that other factors influence at least part of the stock returns as well (such as size, book-to-market value, P/E ratio etc.).[20]

Additionally, criticized is the impossibility to test the CAPM in the real world due to the unrealistic assumptions it is based on.[21] This statement mainly stems out of the problems in defining the right market portfolio. Theoretically, this portfolio should include all asset classes (such as stocks, bonds consumer durables, real estate, etc.), which is practically not realizable. Thus, all market portfolios that are defined to test the CAPM can just be an approximation. Therefore, one can argue that all tests designed to validate the CAPM only analyze the market approximation's efficiency and not the CAPM.[22] On the other hand, there is evidence that the results when testing the CAPM with a market portfolio consisting out of many different asset classes instead of just using stocks do not significantly differ.[23] Furthermore, one can criticize that that the CAPM is generally tested with ex-post data although it is an ex-ante model. The problems arising out of that context are that the ex-post distribution of risk and return often significantly differs from its ex-ante magnitudes[24] and that the betas are not stable over time which causes difficulties when using ex-post data to estimate the future performance of an asset.[25]

Additional points of criticism of the CAPM are based on the underlying assumptions of the model which do not reflect reality efficiently. One can argue that the risk-free rate does not exist in the real world[26] and criticize the one-period world of the CAPM.[27] Although there are extensions of the model which have been developed to deal with these

---

17 See PEROLD (2004), pp. 15-17.
18 See REINGANUM (1981), p. 439.
19 See FAMA/ FRENCH (2004), p. 25.
20 See FAMA/ FRENCH (1992), pp. 427-429.
21 See FAMA/ FRENCH (2004), pp. 41-43.
22 See ROLL (1977), pp. 129-132.
23 See STAMBAUGH (1982), pp. 266f.
24 See FRIEND/ BLUME (1970), pp. 563-565.
25 See MULLINS (1982), p. 112.
26 See BLACK (1972), pp. 446-455.
27 See MERTON (1973), pp. 867f.

problems, most of the CAPM assumptions still reflect an idealized world and just are not able to depict reality.[28] Examples are the assumption of unrestricted risk-free borrowing and lending at a hypothetical risk-free rate, the friction in the market, that the people do not have to pay taxes and that transaction costs do not occur, which all cannot be found in the real world and thus are arguable. Additionally criticized can be that all investors share the same level of information and thus have the same expectation about the distribution of returns, which just does not prove to be true in the real world.

Another point of critique is that testing the CAPM always goes along with testing the market efficiency[29] due to the fact that abnormal returns, which are not corresponding to the CAPM could be either caused by a failure in the model or by the fact that markets are not efficient in a sense that price movements are independent from the available information.[30] An efficient capital market is defined as a market in which security prices rapidly adjust to new information,[31] implying that current security prices reflect all given information about a security.[32] Maurice Kendall (1953) found out that the stock price movements are not dependent on each other[33] and follow a so called random walk.[34] Several studies have been made to find out whether stock markets are efficient, but the results are controversial.[35] However, since other researchers assume that capital markets are efficient in order to be able to make comments about the validity of the CAPM and to interpret their findings, it will also be presumed in the empirical part of this paper that the German stock market is efficient.

Resulting out of all these points one can surely argue that the CAPM has several shortcomings, but although these have been known for decades it still is widely used and a "must" in finance theory for its ability to describe the relationship between risk and return that easily and intuitively

3 Previous Research

Over the last decades the CAPM has gone through extensive empirical testing. Thereby, financial researchers either use cross-sectional or time-series regression to test the validity of the CAPM and to examine whether the relationship between return and risk can

---

28 See MULLINS (1982), p. 112.
29 See JAVED (2000), pp. 20f.
30 See BODIE/ KANE/ MARCUS (2002), pp. 342-358.
31 See REILLY/ BROWN (2003), p. 176.
32 See FAMA (1970), p. 383.
33 See KENDALL (1953), p. 20.
34 See BREALEY/ MYERS (2003), p. 347.

be measured as implied by the model.[36] Overall, both regression approaches lead to a rejection of the model in most of the studies. In some of the earlier tests it was found that the intercept of the regression has a higher value than the risk-free rate and that the risk return relationship is flatter than the CAPM predicts.[37] This leads to the result that cost of equity estimates for low beta stocks are too low and estimates for high beta stocks are too high.[38]

One of the most often cited tests of the CAPM is the study of Black, Jensen and Scholes (1972). In this study the excess returns of the constructed portfolios were regressed on the excess return of the market portfolio. This should normally imply that the intercept term is zero, but this could not be validated. The study indicates that the intercept is positive for low-beta portfolios and negative for high-beta portfolios, which challenges the risk return relationship of the CAPM.[39] Another test by Fama and MacBeth (1973) combined the time-series and the cross-sectional regression approaches. The authors used the time-series approach to estimate the betas of individual stocks and to form 20 portfolios ranked on these. In a second step they used the cross-sectional regression to investigate the slope coefficient and the intercept term.[40] The conclusion of this study states that "[…] there seems to be a positive trade-off between return and risk."[41]

More recent studies generally focus on testing the assumption that beta is the only factor which explains the expected returns. These studies conclude that factors like size, book-to-market value, P/E ratio etc. have a significant statistical influence on the expected returns and thus state that the validity of the CAPM is questionable.[42] But, these studies have then again been challenged empirically and that is why the CAPM debate is still going on.[43]

The studies that have been mentioned so far have all been made on the U.S. stock market. Compared to the many existing empirical tests in the U.S. the empirical record of CAPM tests on the German stock market is quite poor. An empirical study by Sauer and Murphy (1992) on the German market concludes that although the CAPM does not explain the risk-return relationship in all details it is still the best model in order to de-

---

35 See REILLY/ BROWN (2003), pp. 198f.
36 See FAMA/ FRENCH (2004), p. 25.
37 See LINTNER (1965), pp. 13-37; DOUGLAS (1968), pp. 3-45.
38 See FRIEND/ BLUME (1970), p. 571.
39 See BLACK/ JENSEN/ SCHOLES (1972), pp. 112-114.
40 See FAMA/ MACBETH (1973), pp. 614-617.
41 FAMA/ MACBETH (1973), p. 633.
42 See BASU (1977), pp. 663-682; See BASU (1983), pp. 129-156; See FAMA/ FRENCH (1992), pp. 427-429.

scribe the stock returns in Germany.[44] Contradicting this statement, a study by Schlag and Wohlschieß (1997) argues that beta has not got a good explanatory power in predicting returns.[45] But Elsas, El-Shaer and Theissen (2003) do not come to the same result and conclude that there is indeed a positive significant relationship between beta and average returns.[46] Out of these disagreeing studies one can derive the necessity for further studies like this one in order to come up with conclusions about the validity of the CAPM on the German stock market.

4 Empirical Study

4.1 Data

As already mentioned above, this study focuses on examining the validity of the CAPM on the German stock market. Therefore, all the data which is used originates in Germany and is obtained from DataStream. The used data set consists of the monthly total return index of listed German companies for the time period from July 1990 to July 2005. Thus, dividends, stock splits and capital gains are already adjusted for. The total number of securities used is 213, which may seem small compared to other empirical studies about the U.S. market. However, the included stocks of this study cover a large percentage of the whole market capitalization of the German stock market and thus are representative. Since several studies about European markets advice using an interbank offered rate as a proxy for the risk free rate,[47] the monthly FIBOR is being used.

One main point of critique about the validity of empirical studies when testing the CAPM stems from choosing the "right" market portfolio. In theory, this portfolio should contain all risky assets available in the market.[48] However, Stambaugh (1982) has shown that using stocks as a market proxy does not result in significantly different findings than using a market portfolio out of several asset classes[49] and thus, stocks are chosen in this study as well. Most of the original empirical papers testing the CAPM on the American market use the S&P 500 index as a market proxy [50] and therefore this paper will define that the market proxy consists out of the 213 stocks included in the data set to depict the German market.

---

43 See JAGANNATHAN/ MCGRATTAN (1995), pp. 6-17.
44 See SAUER/ MURPHY (1992), p. 194.
45 See SCHLAG/ WOHLSCHIEß (1997), pp. 17f.
46 See ELSAS/ EL-SHAER/ THEISSEN (2003), pp. 16-18.
47 See SAUER/ MURPHY (1992), p. 188.
48 See FAMA/ FRENCH (2004), pp. 25f.
49 See STAMBAUGH (1982), pp. 266f.

4.2 Methodology

The methodology of this empirical test follows the conventional methodology of a time-series regression and a cross-sectional regression previously adapted by Black, Jensen and Scholes (1972)[51], Fama and MacBeth (1973)[52], etc.. This methodology is the standard in empirical tests of the Sharpe-Lintner version of the model.[53]

When testing the CAPM several problems can arise. One of the problems is that a bias can occur due to the systematically higher leverage of financial institutions.[54] Therefore, the banks are excluded in the portfolio building process, which is explained in the following. Another problem which can arise when testing the model is caused by the fact that estimates of betas have to be taken because the true beta coefficients are unobservable.[55] These beta estimates for individual assets are imprecise, because they create a measurement error problem when they are used to explain average returns.[56] This stems due to the fact that the error-term in the regression is not cross-sectionally independent when estimating the betas.[57] As suggested by researchers portfolios of stocks are used instead of individual securities to improve the precision of the beta estimates.[58] These portfolios lead to more accurate results than testing every single stock. The usage of portfolios is valid since the CAPM explains security returns and thus can also explain portfolio returns since expected returns and betas are combined in the same way in portfolios.[59] This statement is underlined with the following formula, which states that the portfolio beta, β_{pM}, is the sum of the weighted, x_{ip}, asset betas, β_{iM}, and the expected return of the portfolio, $E(R_P)$, is the sum of the weighted expected asset returns:

$$\beta_{PM} = \sum_{i=1}^{N} x_{iP}\beta_{iM} \text{ , and } E(R_P) = \sum_{i=1}^{N} x_{iP}E(R_i)$$

The portfolios in this study are formed on pre-ranking betas, as suggested by Black, Jensen and Scholes (1972)[60], in the following way: The starting point is to estimate the betas for all stocks for the five year period August 1990 to July 1995. This is done by using the ordinary least squares (OLS) regression. The monthly returns of the individual

---

50 See BANDOURIAN/ WINKELMANN (2003), p. 91.
51 See BLACK/ JENSEN/ SCHOLES (1972), pp. 79-98.
52 See FAMA/ MACBETH (1973), pp. 614-617.
53 See FAMA/ FRENCH (2004), p. 31.
54 See SCHLAG/ WOHLSCHIEß (1997), p. 4.
55 See BLACK/ JENSEN/ SCHOLES (1972), p. 85.
56 See FAMA/ FRENCH (2004), p. 31.
57 See BLACK/ JENSEN/ SCHOLES (1972), pp. 84f.
58 See BLACK/ JENSEN/ SCHOLES (1972), pp. 84f.
59 See FAMA/ FRENCH (2004), p. 31.

stocks are regressed on the market portfolio using the following equation, which states that the return of an individual asset in time *t*, R_{it}, is explained by the intercept term of the regression, α_i, plus the slope coefficient of the regression, β_i, times the risk premium, which is defined as the market return in time *t*, R_{Mt}, minus the risk free rate in time *t*, R_{ft}:

$$R_{it} = \alpha_i + \beta_i (R_{Mt} - R_{ft})$$

Following, the 200 remaining securities are ranked on the basis of their beta estimates from low to high and are assigned to the portfolios - the lowest ten percent in portfolio one and the highest ten percent in portfolio ten and so on. This implies that portfolio one contains the least risky assets and portfolio ten the riskiest ones. This assignment procedure can generally be done in two ways, the value weight and the equal weight approach. In this case, this study refers on Fama and MacBeth (1973) and thus the equal weight approach is used in this paper as well.[61] Therefore, all returns belonging to one portfolio are added up and then divided by the number of securities in the portfolio, *N*, to come up with the portfolio return, R_P.

$$R_P = \frac{1}{N} \sum_{i=1}^{N} R_i$$

Using this equation, the return of each of the ten portfolios is calculated for each of the next 12 month from August 1995 to July 1996. Following, the entire process is repeated in August of each year, which leads to the result that the composition of the portfolios can change on a yearly basis. Therefore, this procedure "[...] allows for any non-stationarity in the coefficients through time."[62] In this way ten years of monthly returns on ten portfolios for all 200 stocks in the data file are obtained. These monthly returns are then used in the time-series regression, where the monthly excess return of the individual portfolio in time *t*, $\overline{R}_{Pt}$, is regressed on the market excess return in time *t*, $\overline{R}_{Mt}$, by using the following time-series regression formula, where $\hat{\alpha}_P$ is the intercept term for the portfolio in time *t*, $\hat{\beta}_P$ is the slope of the time-series regression and ε_{Pt} is the error term of the regression for the portfolio in time *t*:[63]

$$\overline{R}_{Pt} = \hat{\alpha}_P + \hat{\beta}_P \overline{R}_{Mt} + \varepsilon_{Pt}$$

---

60 See BLACK/ JENSEN/ SCHOLES (1972), pp. 86.

61 See FAMA/ MACBETH (1973), p. 614.

62 BLACK/ JENSEN/ SCHOLES (1972), p. 86.

The CAPM implies that there is a positive relationship between risk and return, which will be defined as hypothesis I. Additionally, it states that the "Jensen's alpha", the intercept term in the time-series regression, is zero for each asset. To underline these statements, which are based on the regression, the calculated coefficients are additionally tested for statistical significance by using the standard t-test. The t-values for the alpha and beta are defined as the ratio of the observed variable divided by its standard error, s:[64]

$$t(\alpha_i) = \frac{\alpha_i}{s(\alpha_i)}$$

Next to the time-series regression a cross-sectional regression is run in order to further underscore the results of this empirical study. In a first step the individual stocks are grouped into portfolios to reduce the bias introduced through the existence of measurement errors in the beta estimates. In fact, exactly the same grouping procedure is used as in the time-series regression above. The cross-sectional parameters are then estimated by using the average monthly portfolio returns, $\overline{R}_P$, and the estimated risk coefficients, $\hat{\beta}_P$, which are obtained from the time-series regression. The following formula is used in the regression, where $\hat{\gamma}_0$ is the intercept term, $\hat{\gamma}_1$ the slope and $\overline{e}_P^*$ the measurement error of the regression:[65]

$$\overline{R}_P = \hat{\gamma}_0 + \hat{\gamma}_1 \hat{\beta}_P + \overline{e}_P^*$$

By using the portfolios as explained above one can virtually eliminate the measurement error problem and thus will yield consistent estimates of the parameters $\hat{\gamma}_0$ and $\hat{\gamma}_1$. Theoretically, $\hat{\gamma}_0$ should equal zero if the CAPM holds, which describes what will be tested as hypothesis II. Furthermore, the CAPM implies that $\hat{\gamma}_1$ should be equal to the monthly excess return of the market, γ_1, which is defined to be hypothesis III. The significance of the cross-sectional regression coefficients is additionally tested by calculating their t-values.

Finally, the results of this empirical study are graphically illustrated by plotting the average excess monthly return and the beta of each portfolio into a risk return diagram. These results are then compared to the estimates, which have been given by the CAPM to see whether the model was able to predict the risk-return relationship.

---

63 See FAMA/ FRENCH (2004), p. 32.
64 See JENSEN (1972), p. 364.

4.3 Results, Interpretations and Findings

Given the ten years of monthly returns and the least squares estimates on each of the ten portfolios calculated as explained above, the results of the time-series regression are shown in table I. Portfolio 1 contains the 10% least risky assets and portfolio 10 contains the riskiest securities. The estimated risk coefficients, $\hat{\beta}$, range from 0,14993 in portfolio 1 to 1,03775 in portfolio 10. The second line of the table shows the intercept term of the regression, $\hat{\alpha}$, which is tested for significance with the student-t test. The results of this test are depicted in the third line of the table. The next line shows the correlation between the monthly average excess returns of the market and the monthly average excess returns of the portfolios. The correlation rises in a nearly straight way from 0,23317 in portfolio 1 to 0,81503 in portfolio 10. The last two lines in the table show the monthly average excess return of the portfolios and the standard deviation of it.

When looking at the results for the betas in table I, the first thing to note, next to the nearly linear increase from portfolio 1 to portfolio 10, is that nine out of ten portfolios have a beta of less than one, which could be the result of the fact that most of the securities with a high market capitalisation have a high beta and thus group in portfolio 10. This is also underlined by the correlation values which clearly show a positive relation with the beta coefficients. One can additionally note that the standard deviation of the monthly average excess return rises from portfolio 1 to portfolio 10 as expected since the standard deviation is as well a risk coefficient as beta. One of the most important things to notice in this table is that there is a slight increase in the average monthly excess return from portfolio 1 to portfolio 10, which can be seen more clearly in the results of the cross-sectional regression. This implies that the risk return relationship is generally positive and thus partly confirms hypothesis I. But, one should also have a look at the average monthly excess return of the market, which clearly outperforms all of the portfolios. Next to these findings one should note that the alpha intercepts tend to be positive for the low beta portfolios and tend to be negative for the high beta portfolios. This implies on the one hand that the high-risk securities earned less on average than predicted by the traditional form of the CAPM and on the other one that the low-risk securities earned more than predicted by the model. But, when drawing that conclusion one should mention that none of the t-values in table I is greater than 1,5. Thus all the intercepts are not significantly different from zero, as it is implied by the model.

[65] See BLACK/ JENSEN/ SCHOLES (1972), p. 92.

But, as Black Jensen and Scholes (1972) state, one should pay attention when interpreting these t-values since the normality assumptions can be questioned.[66]

Additionally, the cross-sectional regression is calculated as explained previously based on the results of the time-series regression. Using the cross-sectional regression the least squares estimates between the average monthly excess return and the portfolio betas have been calculated. The results of this regression are plotted into a risk-return diagram. Figure II shows the results for the whole period. The dots represent the portfolios and the square depicts the market portfolio. The dotted line (Portfolio Slope) shows the least squares estimate of the relation between risk and return of the portfolios and the other line (Market Slope) points out the relationship as implied by the CAPM.

Figure II: Average excess monthly returns versus systematic risk for the 10-year period 8.1995-7.2005

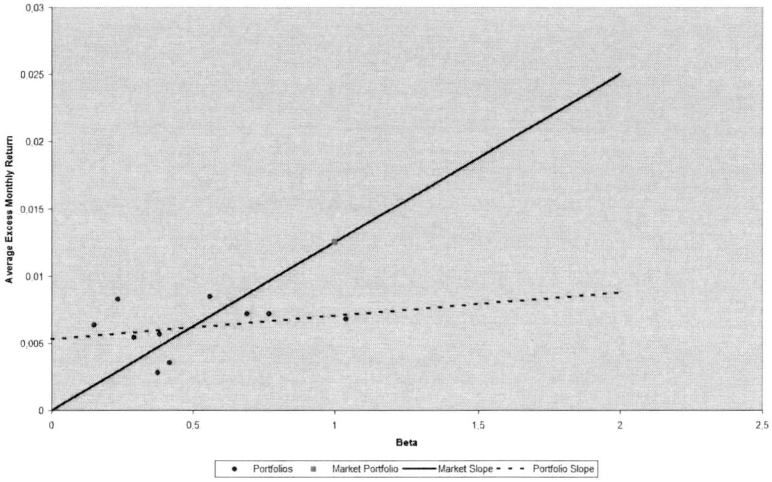

Nearly all of the critical statements that have been made for the time-series regression can also be seen in the figure. For the whole period one has to note that the risk return relationship is generally positive, but flatter than predicted by the model. This implies that hypothesis III has to be rejected. Additionally, the intercept seems to differ from zero, which leads to a rejection of hypothesis II. These results are summarized and underlined with significance in table II. Therefore, one generally has to conclude that the explanation power of the CAPM on the German stock market has to be questioned. But,

66 See BLACK/ JENSEN/ SCHOLES (1972), p. 95.

some caution should be used when analyzing the t-values in table II since they overstate the significance of the results due to a high fluctuation of the estimated coefficients in the subperiods.[67]

In order to test the stationarity of the empirical relations the whole period has been divided into four sub periods each containing 30 month, August 1995 to January 1998, February 1998 to July 2000, August 2000 to January 2003, February 2003 to July 2005. Table III and the figures III-VI summarize the results for all of the four subperiods in addition to what is presented in table II. Table III shows the beta, the alpha and the t-values of alpha for each period and each portfolio. Additionally the average monthly excess return and its standard deviation for each portfolio in each period are depicted. The figures use the same graphical method as figure II.

Analyzing table III, one can see that the beta coefficients seem to be stationary over time in some of the portfolios, e.g. portfolio 9, but in some of the others they are defiantly not stationary over time, e.g. portfolio 2. Another point to note is that the betas of the portfolios in the subperiods do not rise in a straight way from portfolio 1 to portfolio 10 as in the whole period. In addition, none of the portfolios in period one and two have a beta of one or higher. These findings could be caused by a combination of the market capitalization allocation described earlier and the short time period that is being tested. Another point to notice is that all portfolios have a negative monthly average excess return in the third period which seems to be caused by the burst of the tech bubble.

The main result in period one is that the CAPM underestimated nine out of ten portfolios. This is indicated by the negative alphas in table III and illustrated by figure III. The finding for the alpha values for the whole period, just hold in one of the four subperiods, period two. The existence of positive intercepts for the low-risk portfolios and negative intercepts for the high-risk portfolios in this period leads to an underestimation of the low-risk securities and an overestimation of the high-risk securities, which can also be seen in figure IV. This is the only figure in which the portfolio slope (negative slope) does not go into the same direction as predicted by the CAPM (positive slope), which strongly contradicts to the model. As in period two, risk did not get rewarded during period three since the slopes of both lines in figure V are negative which is caused by the burst of the tech bubble. Additionally, one can see in table III that the intercepts for period three are, as in period one, all negative except one. As stated above, this implies, as shown in figure V, that the CAPM generally predicted higher average returns than

---

[67] See BLACK/ JENSEN/ SCHOLES (1972), p. 98.

actually earned by the portfolios. This finding is underlined by some significance as stated in the t-values for the alphas in table III. Contrarily, in period four all the intercepts are positive, which vice versa implies that the CAPM underestimated the average return for all portfolios in period four which is shown in table III and figure VI. This finding is particularly important since six of the ten intercepts are statistically significant. The reason for that can be found in the effects of the burst of the tech bubble on the beta estimation period.

Overall, the results of the subperiods further challenge the CAPM since hypothesis I can just be validated in the subperiods one and four, hypothesis II, has to be rejected in all periods except period two and hypothesis III cannot be confirmed at all.

5 Summary and Conclusion

The main goal of this paper was, as defined in the beginning, to analyze the relationship between risk and return on the German stock market to find out whether the CAPM holds. As stated above, the success of the CAPM mainly stems out of the fact that the model is easy to understand and that it offers intuitively pleasing predictions about the relation between risk and return. But, the empirical record of the CAPM shows that the model has never been a real empirical success on the international stock market and this is what this paper has to conclude as well.

Using a time-series and a cross-sectional regression the paper shows as its main result that the relationship between beta and average excess returns over the ten year testing period is generally positive, but flatter than predicted by the model. Additionally shown is that the alpha values tend to be positive for low risk securities and negative for high risk securities. Thus, these alphas lead to the effect that the CAPM tends to overestimate high-risk securities and tends to underestimate low-risk securities. In order to test the stationarity of the empirical relations the ten year testing period has been divided into four subperiods. Since the empirical results of the subperiods have further challenged the ability of the CAPM to predict the returns, the study comes to the conclusion that the explanatory power of the CAPM for the German stock market is questionable. The fact that similar results have been found in other studies, as pointed out in chapter three, additionally validates the evidence.

Overall, this leads to the question if the CAPM is the right model to be used in such a wide field of applications as pointed out in the beginning, which could be an interesting starting point for further studies.

Appendix

List of Figures

List of Tables

Table I: Summary of Statistics for Time Series Tests, Entire Period

Item	Portfolio Number				
	1	2	3	4	5
$\hat{\beta}$	0,14993	0,23182	0,28987	0,37360	0,38121
$\hat{\alpha}$	0,00450	0,00539	0,00181	-0,00190	0,00091
$t(\hat{\alpha})$	1,26773	1,45878	0,57562	-0,61267	0,27592
$r(\bar{R},\bar{R}_M)$	0,23317	0,33546	0,46358	0,56419	0,54979
$\bar{R}$	0,00638	0,00829	0,00544	0,00278	0,00568
$\sigma_{\bar{R}}$	0,03897	0,04189	0,03790	0,04014	0,04203

Table I: (Continued)

Item	Portfolio Number					
	6	7	8	9	10	$\bar{R}_M$
$\hat{\beta}$	0,41920	0,55977	0,69092	0,77000	1,03775	1,00000
$\hat{\alpha}$	-0,00171	0,00148	-0,00143	-0,00243	-0,00619	
$t(\hat{\alpha})$	-0,53547	0,41868	-0,39845	-0,70362	-1,47737	
$r(\bar{R},\bar{R}_M)$	0,59752	0,66872	0,73746	0,78449	0,81503	
$\bar{R}$	0,00354	0,00849	0,00722	0,00721	0,00680	0,01252
$\sigma_{\bar{R}}$	0,04252	0,05074	0,05679	0,05949	0,07717	0,06061

Note:

Entire period: 8.1995–7.2005.

Sample size for each regression: 120.

Table II: Summary of Cross-sectional Regression Coefficients and Their t-Values

	Time Period				
	Total Period	Subperiods			
	8.1995-7.2005	8.1995-1.1998	2.1998-7.2000	8.2000-1.2003	2.2003-7.2005
$\hat{\gamma}_0$	0,00533	0,00326	0,00847	-0,01193	0,02046
$\hat{\gamma}_1$	0,00174	0,00896	-0,00641	-0,00267	0,00631
γ_1	0,01252	0,02272	0,01881	-0,01213	0,02068
$t(\hat{\gamma}_0)$	4,10071***	1,21187	2,96232***	-4,17904***	6,52575***
$t(\gamma_1 - \hat{\gamma}_1)$	4,60456***	3,22998***	4,15397***	-1,94273*	2,51915**

*denotes significance at 10%, **5%, ***1%

Where $t(\gamma_1 - \hat{\gamma}_1)$ is calculated as: $$t(\gamma_1 - \hat{\gamma}_1) = \frac{\gamma_1 - \hat{\gamma}_1}{s(\hat{\gamma}_1)}$$

Table III: Summary of Statistics for Time Series Tests, Subperiods

		Portfolio Number				
Item	Sub-period	1	2	3	4	5
$\hat{\beta}$	1	0,18856	0,29267	0,39455	0,58138	0,52915
	2	0,09629	0,08818	0,01389	0,27602	0,27634
	3	0,12373	0,28542	0,33941	0,31944	0,31399
	4	0,08647	0,08984	0,34199	0,48199	0,46380
$\hat{\alpha}$	1	-0,00154	-0,00129	-0,00342	-0,00754	-0,00298
	2	0,01095	0,01389	0,00160	0,00113	0,00239
	3	-0,01003	-0,01186	-0,00049	-0,01321	-0,00727
	4	0,01974	0,02572	0,00899	0,00913	0,00758
$t(\hat{\alpha})$	1	-0,52704	-0,21840	-0,43634	-1,24193	-0,48897
	2	1,49253	1,59774	0,23501	0,19677	0,26554
	3	-1,49172	-2,85258***	-0,09444	-2,03529*	-1,25568
	4	1,97705*	2,73061**	1,82050*	1,30424	1,29869
$\overline{R}$	1	0,00275	0,00536	0,00554	0,00567	0,00904
	2	0,01276	0,01555	0,00186	0,00632	0,00758
	3	-0,01153	-0,01532	-0,00461	-0,01709	-0,01108
	4	0,02153	0,02757	0,01896	0,01620	0,01717
$\sigma_{\overline{R}}$	1	0,01629	0,03112	0,04147	0,03899	0,03754
	2	0,03831	0,04517	0,03507	0,03441	0,04960
	3	0,03680	0,03029	0,03689	0,04155	0,03829
	4	0,05021	0,04741	0,03572	0,03953	0,03832

*denotes significance at 10%, **5%, ***1%

Note:

Subperiods: Subperiod 1: 8.1995-1.1998;

Subperiod 2: 2.1998-7.2000;

Subperiod 3: 8.2000-1.2003;

Subperiod 4: 2.2003-7.2005

Sample size for each regression: 30.

Table III continues on the following page.

Table III: (Continued)

Item	Sub-period	Portfolio Number 6	7	8	9	10	$\overline{R}_M$
$\hat{\beta}$	1	0,49581	0,65355	0,86741	0,83345	0,98240	1,00000
	2	0,32739	0,42114	0,71642	0,72707	0,84856	1,00000
	3	0,39574	0,57950	0,68605	0,72481	1,23716	1,00000
	4	0,39454	0,56025	0,55701	0,78846	1,02047	1,00000
$\hat{\alpha}$	1	0,00147	-0,00432	-0,01000	-0,00337	-0,01451	
	2	-0,00824	-0,00095	-0,01315	-0,00988	-0,00867	
	3	-0,01344	-0,00620	0,00033	-0,00937	-0,00036	
	4	0,01358	0,01810	0,01532	0,01133	0,00640	
$t(\hat{\alpha})$	1	0,23387	-0,58114	-1,61361	-0,49120	-1,17655	
	2	-1,28857	-0,13988	-1,66590	-1,42196	-1,45142	
	3	-1,96935*	-1,22018	0,04882	-1,48073	-0,05542	
	4	2,19626**	1,96796*	1,83421*	1,35471	0,73658	
$\overline{R}$	1	0,01273	0,01052	0,00970	0,01557	0,00781	0,02272
	2	-0,00209	0,00697	0,00033	0,00379	0,00729	0,01881
	3	-0,01824	-0,01323	-0,00800	-0,01816	-0,01538	-0,01213
	4	0,02174	0,02968	0,02684	0,02763	0,02750	0,02068
$\sigma_{\overline{R}}$	1	0,03740	0,04609	0,04887	0,04968	0,07360	0,04480
	2	0,03904	0,04426	0,06120	0,05862	0,06231	0,06382
	3	0,04625	0,05003	0,06139	0,06250	0,09653	0,07274
	4	0,03747	0,05134	0,05494	0,05942	0,06978	0,05346

*denotes significance at 10%, **5%, ***1%

Note:

Subperiods: Subperiod 1: 8.1995-1.1998;

Subperiod 2: 2.1998-7.2000;

Subperiod 3: 8.2000-1.2003;

Subperiod 4: 2.2003-7.2005

Sample size for each regression: 30.

Figure III: Average excess monthly returns versus systematic risk for the 2,5-year period 8.1995-1.1998

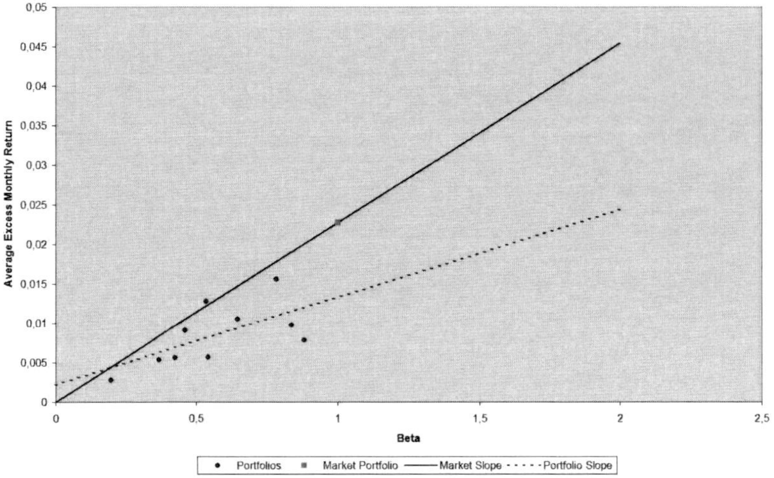

Figure IV: Average excess monthly returns versus systematic risk for the 2,5-year period 2.1998-7.2000

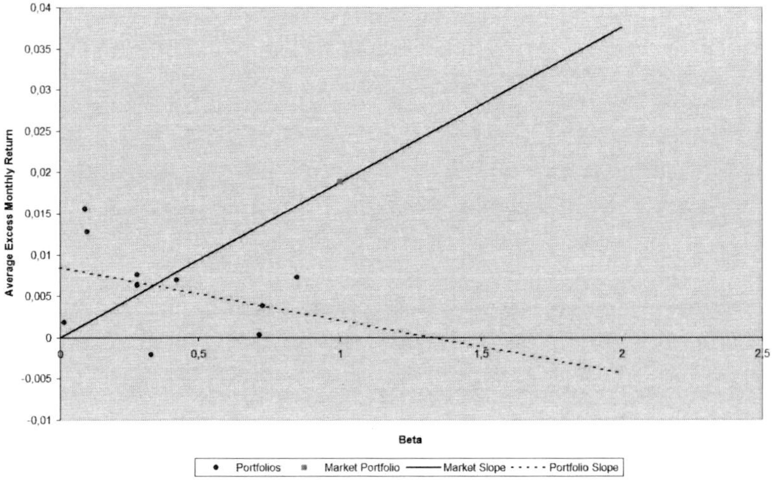

Figure V: Average excess monthly returns versus systematic risk for the 2,5-year period 8.2000-1.2003

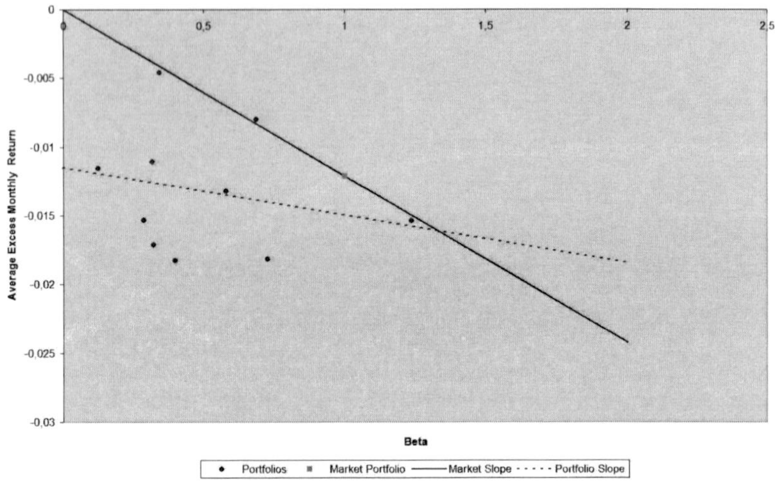

Figure VI: Average excess monthly returns versus systematic risk for the 2,5-year period 2.2003-7.2005

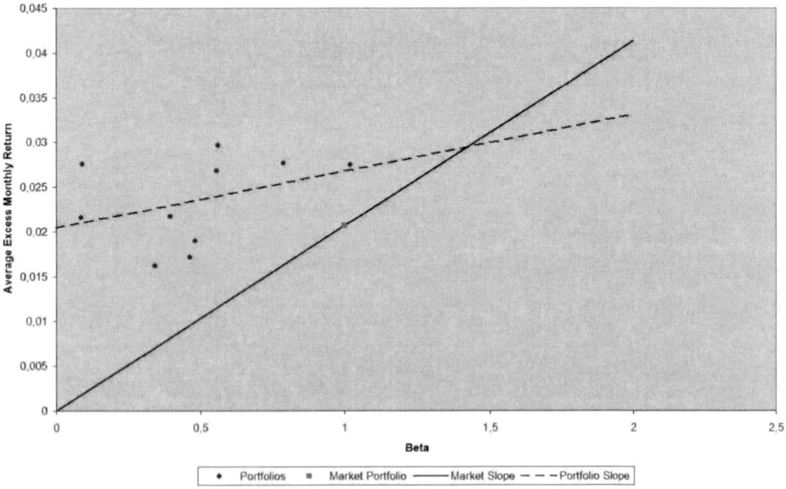

References

BANDOURIAN, RIPSY / WINKELMANN, KURT (2003): The Market Portfolio, in: Littermann, Bob (ed.): Modern Investment Management – An Equilibrium Approach, New York, pp. 91-103.

BANZ, ROLF W. (1981): The Relationship between Return and Market Value of Common Stocks, in: Journal of Financial Economics, 1981, Vol. 9, No. 1/1981, pp. 3-18.

BASU, SANJOY (1977): Investment Performance of Common Stocks in Relation to their Price-Earnings Ratios: A Test of the Efficient Market Hypothesis, in: The Journal of Finance, 1977, Vol. 32, No. 3/1977, pp. 663-682.

BASU, SANJOY (1983): The Relationship between Earnings' Yield, Market Value and Return for NYSE Common Stocks – Further Evidence, in: Journal of Financial Economics, 1983, Vol. 12, No. 1/1983, pp. 129-156.

BLACK, FISCHER (1972): Capital Market Equilibrium with Restricted Borrowing, in: The Journal of Business, Vol. 45, No. 3/1972, pp. 444-455.

BLACK, FISCHER / JENSEN, MICHAEL C. / SCHOLES, MYRON (1972): The Capital Asset Pricing Model: Some Empirical Tests, in: Jensen, Michael C. (ed.): Studies in the Theory of Capital Markets, New York, pp. 79-121.

BODIE, ZVI / KANE, ALEX / MARCUS, ALAN J. (2002): Investments, 5th revised and ex-tended Edition, New York.

BREALEY, RICHARD A. / MYERS, STEWART C. (2003): Principles of Corporate Finance, 7th revised and extended Edition, New York.

DOUGLAS, GEORGE W. (1968): Risk in the Equity Market: An empirical Appraisal of Market Efficiency, in: Yale Economic Essays, Vol. 9, pp. 3-45.

ELSAS, RALF / EL-SHAER, MAHMOUD / THEISSEN, ERIK (2003): Beta and returns revisited – Evidence from the German stock market, in: Journal of International Financial Markets, Institutions & Money, Vol. 13, No. 1/2003, pp. 1-18.

FAMA, EUGENE F. (1970): Efficient Capital Markets: A Review of Theory and Empirical Work, in: The Journal of Finance, 1970, Vol. 25, No. 2/1970, pp. 383-417.

FAMA, EUGENE F. (1996): Multifactor Portfolio Efficiency and Multifactor Asset Pricing, in: Journal of Financial and Quantitative Analysis, 1996, Vol. 31, No. 4/1996, pp. 441-465.

FAMA, EUGENE F. / FRENCH, KENNETH R. (1992): The Cross-Section of Expected Stock Returns, in: The Journal of Finance, Vol. 47, No. 2/1992, pp. 427-465.

FAMA, EUGENE F. / FRENCH, KENNETH R. (2004): The Capital Asset Pricing Model: Theory and Evidence, in: Journal of Economic Perspective, Vol. 18, No. 3/2004, pp. 25-46.

FAMA, EUGENE, F. / MACBETH, JAMES D. (1973): Risk, Return, and Equilibrium: Empirical Tests, in: Journal of Political Economy, Vol. 81, No. 3/1973, pp. 607-636.

FRIEND, IRVIN / BLUME, MARSHALL E. (1970): Measurement of Portfolio Performance Under Uncertainty, in: American Economic Review, Vol. 60, No. 4/1970, pp. 561-575.

GRAHAM, JOHN R. / HARVEY CAMPBELL R. (2001): Expectations of Equity Risk Premia: Volatility and Asymmetry from a Corporate Finance Perspective, in: NBER Working Papers 8678, National Bureau of Economic Research, pp.187-244.

JAGANNATHAN, RAVI / MCGRATTAN, ELLEN R. (1995): The CAPM Debate, in: Federal Reserve Bank of Minneapolis Quarterly Review, Vol. 19, No. 4, pp. 2-17.

JAGANNATHAN, RAVI / WANG, RAVI (1996): The Conditional CAPM and the Cross-Section of Expected Returns, in: The Journal of Finance, Vol. 51, No. 1/1996, pp. 3-53.

JAVED, ATTIYA Y. (2000): Alternative Capital Asset Pricing Models: A Review of Theory and Evidence, Research Report No. 179, Pakistan Institute of Development Economics (PIDE).

JENSEN, MICHAEL C. (1972): Capital Markets: Theory and Evidence, in: Bell Journal of Economics & Management Science, 1972, Vol. 3, No. 2/1972, pp. 357-398.

KENDALL, MAURICE G. (1953): The Analysis of Economic Time Series, Part I. Prices, in: Journal of the Royal Statistical Society, 1953, pp. 11-25.

LINTNER, JOHN (1965): The Valuation of Risk Assets and Selection of Risky Investments in Stock Portfolio and Capital Budgeting, in: The Review of Financial Studies, Vol. 47, No. 1/1965, pp. 13-37.

MARKOWITZ, HARRY (1952): Portfolio Selection, in: The Journal of Finance, Vol. 7, No. 1/1952, pp. 77-91.

MERTON, ROBERT C. (1973): An Intertemporal Asset Pricing Model, in: Econometrica, Vol. 41, No. 5/1973, pp. 867-887.

MULLINS, DAVID W. JR. (1982): Does the capital asset pricing model work?, in: Harvard Business Review, January-February 1982, pp. 105-114.

PEROLD, ANDRÉ F. (2004): The Capital Asset Pricing Model, in: Journal of Economic Perspective, Vol. 18, No. 3/2004, pp. 3-24.

REILLY, FRANK K. / BROWN, KEITH C. (2003): Investment Analysis and Portfolio Management, 7th revised and extended Edition, Mason.

REINGANUM, MARC R. (1981): A new empirical perspective on the CAPM, in Journal of Financial and Quantitative Analysis, Vol. 16, No.4/1981, pp. 439-462.

ROLL, RICHARD (1977): A Critique of the Asset Pricing Theory's Tests – Part I: On Past and Potential Testability of the Theory, in: Journal of Financial Economics, Vol. 4, No. 2/1977, pp. 129-176.

SAUER, ANDREAS / MURPHY, AUSTIN (1992): An empirical comparison of alternative models of capital asset pricing in Germany, in: Journal of Banking and Finance, Vol. 16, No. 1/1992, pp. 183-196.

SCHLAG, CHRISTIAN / WOHLSCHIEß, VOLKER (1997): Is beta dead? Results for the German Stock Market, Working Paper, pp. 1-21.

SHARPE, WILLIAM F. (1964): Capital Asset Prices: A Theory of Market Equilibrium under Conditions of Risk, in: The Journal of Finance, Vol. 14, No. 3/1964, pp. 425-442.

STAMBAUGH, ROBERT (1982): On the Exclusion of Assets from Tests of the Two-Parameter Model – A Sensitivity Analysis, in: Journal of Financial Economics, Vol. 10, No.3/1982, pp. 237-268.